UPSKILLING 101

*A Practical Guide to Building Employee
Skills and Boosting Business Performance*

Michael Watson

This book is dedicated to Ashutosh Garg, Varun Kacholia and Kamal Ahluwalia. You believed in me and I am forever grateful. Here's to all of us enabling the right career for everyone in the world.
-Michael

CONTENTS

Title Page

Dedication

ForeworD

Chapter 1 - Upskilling 101   1

Chapter 2 - The Benefits of Upskilling   4

Chapter 3 - Identifying Skills Gaps in Your Organization   7

Chapter 4 -   How Artificial Intelligence is Helping   12
Organizations Identify the Skills Gap

Chapter 5 - The Role of Managers and Leaders in Upskilling   16

Chapter 6 - Designing Effective Training Programs   20

Chapter 7 - Measuring the ROI of Upskilling   25

Chapter 8 - Overcoming Obstacles to Upskilling   30

Chapter 9 - The Future of Upskilling   41

Chapter 10 - Closing Thoughts   46

About The Author   49

Books By This Author   51

FOREWORD

In today's rapidly changing job market, companies and employees alike face the challenge of keeping up with the latest tools and technologies. As technology continues to advance, many jobs are changing or becoming obsolete, and it can be difficult to keep pace with these changes. That's where upskilling comes in.

Upskilling refers to the process of teaching employees new skills or enhancing existing skills to help them become more effective in their roles. By investing in upskilling programs, companies can ensure that their employees have the skills they need to succeed in their jobs and contribute to the organization's success.

But upskilling is not just important for companies; it's also crucial for employees themselves. In today's job market, it's not enough to have a basic set of skills and qualifications. To succeed and advance in one's career, it's essential to continuously learn and develop new skills. This is where upskilling comes in: it provides employees with the opportunity to enhance their skills and knowledge, and to stay relevant in a rapidly changing job market.

In this book, we explore the importance of upskilling and the ways in which companies are investing in their employees' development. We start by defining upskilling and discussing the key differences between upskilling and reskilling. We then delve into the four main reasons why upskilling is crucial in today's job market:

Rapid Technological Change: Technology is advancing at an unprecedented pace, and many jobs are changing or becoming obsolete as a result. Upskilling helps employees keep pace with these changes and adapt to new tools and technologies.

Skills Gaps: Many organizations face a gap between the skills they need and the skills their employees currently possess. Upskilling can help bridge this gap and ensure that employees have the necessary skills to perform their jobs effectively.

Increased Competition for Talent: As the job market becomes more competitive, companies need to offer opportunities for career growth and development to attract and retain top talent. Upskilling programs can help create a culture of continuous learning and show employees that their company values their growth and development.
Improved Business Performance: Upskilling can lead to increased productivity, efficiency, and innovation, which can have a positive impact on a company's bottom line. By investing in their employees' skills, companies can improve business outcomes and stay ahead of the competition.

Throughout the book, we provide examples of companies that are leading the way in upskilling, as well as best practices and strategies for implementing successful upskilling programs. We also explore the benefits of upskilling for employees, such as increased job satisfaction, career growth, and opportunities for advancement.

Whether you are an employer looking to invest in your employees' development or an employee seeking to enhance your skills and advance your career, this book provides valuable insights and guidance on the importance of upskilling in today's job market. We hope it inspires you to take action and invest in your own growth and development, and that of your organization.

Sincerely,

Michael Watson

CHAPTER 1 - UPSKILLING 101

In today's rapidly changing job market, skills intelligence and upskilling have become critical topics for both employers and employees. In this chapter, we will define skills intelligence and upskilling, discuss their importance, and provide an overview of the book's content.

Definition of Skills Intelligence

Skills intelligence refers to the ability to identify, acquire, and apply new skills and knowledge to remain competitive in the job market. It involves understanding which skills are in demand and being able to develop those skills to meet the needs of employers. Skills intelligence also encompasses the ability to recognize transferable skills, which can be applied to new roles or industries.

Definition of Upskilling

Upskilling is the process of acquiring new skills or enhancing existing ones to improve job performance and remain competitive in the job market. Upskilling can involve training programs, workshops, certifications, or other forms of education that help employees develop the skills needed to succeed in their roles.

Importance of Upskilling in Today's Job Market

In today's job market, the demand for new skills is constantly evolving, driven by technological advancements, changes in consumer behavior, and other factors. As a result, employees who fail to upskill may find themselves left behind, while those who invest in their skills intelligence can remain competitive and increase their career opportunities.

Moreover, upskilling is becoming increasingly important for employers as well. Companies that fail to invest in their employees' development risk losing top talent and falling behind their competitors. By providing opportunities for upskilling, companies can improve employee retention, productivity, and innovation.

Overview of the Book's Content

In this book, we will explore the importance of upskilling and skills intelligence in today's job market. We will provide insights into the latest trends in upskilling, including the different types of programs and training methods available. We will also examine the benefits of upskilling for both employees and employers, as well as the challenges and barriers that can prevent successful upskilling initiatives.

The book will be divided into a series of sections covering:
- The Benefits of Upskilling
- Identifying Skills Gaps in Your Organization
- How AI can help you Identify Skills Gap
- The Role of Managers and Leaders in Upskilling
- Designing Effective Training Programs
- The Role of Technology in Upskilling
- Measuring the ROI of Upskilling
- Overcoming Obstacles to Upskilling
- The Future of Upskilling
- Case Studies: Successful Upskilling Programs

Each section will provide practical advice and real-world examples of successful upskilling initiatives. By the end of the book, readers will have a comprehensive understanding of the importance of upskilling and skills intelligence in today's job market, as well as the tools and strategies needed to implement successful upskilling programs.

CHAPTER 2 - THE BENEFITS OF UPSKILLING

Upskilling is the process of developing new skills or enhancing existing ones to stay competitive in the job market. This chapter will explore the benefits of upskilling, including increased productivity and efficiency, improved employee retention, enhanced job satisfaction and career advancement opportunities, and greater adaptability to changing business needs.

Increased productivity and efficiency

One of the main benefits of upskilling is increased productivity and efficiency in the workplace. When employees have the skills and knowledge they need to perform their jobs well, they can work more efficiently and effectively. This results in higher quality work, faster turnaround times, and increased output. Additionally, upskilling can lead to the adoption of new technologies and processes that can streamline workflows and improve overall productivity.

Improved employee retention

Another benefit of upskilling is improved employee retention. When employees feel that they are developing their skills and advancing their careers, they are more likely to stay with their employer. This is especially true for younger workers who prioritize learning and growth opportunities. By investing in upskilling, organizations can create a more engaged and motivated workforce, which can lead to lower turnover rates and reduced costs associated with recruiting and training new employees.

Enhanced job satisfaction and career advancement opportunities

Upskilling can also lead to enhanced job satisfaction and career advancement opportunities. When employees feel that they are growing and developing professionally, they are more likely to feel fulfilled in their jobs. Additionally, upskilling can open up new career paths and opportunities for advancement, which can lead to higher job satisfaction and increased retention. By investing in upskilling, organizations can create a culture that supports employee growth and development, which can help attract and retain top talent.

Greater adaptability to changing business needs

Finally, upskilling can help organizations become more adaptable to changing business needs. In today's fast-paced and constantly evolving business environment, organizations must be able to quickly adapt to new technologies, processes, and market conditions. By investing in upskilling, organizations can ensure that their employees have the skills and knowledge they need to stay ahead of the curve. This can help organizations respond to changing business needs more quickly and effectively, which can lead to greater success and competitiveness in the marketplace.

Overall, upskilling can have a range of benefits for both organizations and employees. By investing in upskilling, organizations can create a more engaged and productive workforce, which can lead to increased profitability and competitiveness. Additionally, upskilling can help employees develop new skills, enhance their job satisfaction, and advance their careers, which can lead to increased retention and higher job performance.

CHAPTER 3 - IDENTIFYING SKILLS GAPS IN YOUR ORGANIZATION

In order to effectively upskill your workforce, it's important to first identify the areas where your employees are lacking in skills and knowledge. This chapter will explore methods for identifying skills gaps, tools for assessing current employee skills and knowledge, and provide examples of common skills gaps in different industries.

Identifying Skills Gaps in Your Organization

Identifying skills gaps in your organization is crucial for effective upskilling initiatives. Here are some methods for identifying skills gaps:

Conducting a Skills Gap Analysis

A skills gap analysis is a process of identifying the difference between the skills that employees currently have and the skills that are required to meet the needs of the business. There are several methods organizations can use to identify skills gaps. One of the most effective ways is to conduct a comprehensive skills assessment. This involves evaluating the current skills and knowledge of employees and identifying areas where they need improvement. Other methods include analyzing job descriptions, conducting surveys, and examining employee performance data.This analysis can be conducted in several ways, such as:

- Conducting surveys and interviews with employees and managers to determine the current level of skills and knowledge - what skills are necessary to make sure you do not lose market share to your competition.

- Analyzing job descriptions and performance evaluations to determine the required skills and knowledge for each role - is there an opportunity to highlight the new skills you're looking for, both internally and externally

- Analyzing industry trends and changes to determine the future skills and knowledge requirements - where is the market going so you're not left behind (think about the companies who didn't get it right - for example, Blackberry, Blockbuster or Kodak)

Monitoring Performance Metrics

Performance metrics can also help identify skills gaps in your organization. For example, if certain departments or employees consistently fall short of performance targets, it may indicate a skills gap that needs to be addressed. Similarly, if certain types of errors or mistakes are occurring frequently, it may indicate a need for additional training or skills development.

Tools for Assessing Current Employee Skills and Knowledge

There are many tools available for assessing employee skills and knowledge. Some of the most common include competency frameworks, skills assessments, and performance appraisals. Many organizations also use online learning platforms that provide employees with access to training and development resources. Once skills gaps have been identified, the next step is to assess the current skills and knowledge of employees. Here are some tools that can be used for this purpose:

Skills Assessment Tests

Skills assessment tests can be used to evaluate the current skills and knowledge of employees. These tests can be designed to assess specific skills or competencies required for the job, or to assess a more general set of skills that are relevant to the industry.

Performance Evaluations

Performance evaluations can also provide insight into the skills and knowledge of employees. By evaluating employee performance against specific performance goals and objectives, managers can identify areas where additional skills or training may be needed.

Examples of Common Skills Gaps in Different Industries

Skills gaps can vary depending on the industry and the specific needs of the business. Here are some examples of common skills gaps in different industries:

Healthcare

In the healthcare industry, common skills gaps include:
- Knowledge of new medical technologies and treatments
- Communication and interpersonal skills for working with patients and families
- Leadership and management skills for supervisory positions

Technology

In the technology industry, common skills gaps include:

- Knowledge of new programming languages and technologies
- Data analysis and visualization skills
- Cybersecurity and information security skills

Manufacturing

In the manufacturing industry, common skills gaps include:
- Technical skills for working with complex machinery and equipment
- Knowledge of lean manufacturing principles and process improvement techniques
- Leadership and management skills for supervisory positions

As you can see, there are several examples of common skills gaps in different industries and as you can see, the specific skills gaps that exist in different industries can vary widely. However, there are some common skills gaps that cut across all industries. These would include:

Digital literacy:

Many employees lack the digital skills required to work effectively in today's technology-driven workplace forcing employers to bring in outside consultants and contractors to perform jobs that could be done with employees who were upskilled, saving your organization thousands (eventually millions) of dollars over time.

Communication skills:

Effective communication is critical in all industries, but many employees struggle with verbal and written communication.

Leadership skills:

As organizations become more complex and global, there is an increasing need for strong leaders who can manage diverse teams and navigate complex business environments. This is where cultural upskilling become critical for the success of your organization.

Technical skills:

In industries such as healthcare and engineering, technical skills are essential. However, many employees lack the specific technical skills required for their roles. As new technology is introduced, companies are oftentimes forced to hire new employees and say goodbye to those who don't have the skills to transfer. Don't we owe it to our employees, who have worked so hard for us over the years, to do better?

Overall, identifying skills gaps is a critical first step in developing an effective upskilling program. By understanding where employees need to improve, organizations can create targeted training and development initiatives that meet their specific needs.

Conclusion

Identifying skills gaps is an essential step in designing effective upskilling programs. By using methods such as conducting a skills gap analysis and monitoring performance metrics, businesses can identify the specific skills and knowledge areas that need to be addressed. Tools such as skills assessment tests and performance evaluations can help assess the current skills and knowledge of employees. Finally, examples of common skills gaps in different industries can provide insights into the specific skills that may need to be developed in different job roles.

CHAPTER 4 - HOW ARTIFICIAL INTELLIGENCE IS HELPING ORGANIZATIONS IDENTIFY THE SKILLS GAP

As we can clearly see, the skills gap has become a pressing issue for many organizations, as they struggle to keep up with the changing demands of the modern workforce. As previously discussed, rapid technological advances and shifting economic trends have led to a situation where many employees lack the skills needed to succeed in their roles. We know that identifying the skills gap is the first step to addressing the issue, but for many of us, it can be a daunting task, especially for larger organizations with many employees. Fortunately, artificial intelligence (AI) is providing an easier way. With new AI tools and methods for identifying the skills gap and helping organizations bridge it, organizations can identify the gap in skills in hours compared to months. Being able to quickly identify your gaps is oftentimes the difference between thriving as an organization or being forced to close the doors to your business.

AI Methods for Identifying the Skills Gap

As we discussed in the previous chapter, there are several methods for identifying the skills gap within an organization, including surveys, performance evaluations, and job analysis. However, these traditional methods can be time-consuming, expensive, and subject to biases. AI-powered solutions are providing more efficient and accurate ways to identify skills gaps, allowing organizations to focus their resources on targeted training and development.

One method that has gained popularity is the use of big data analytics to identify skills gaps. By analyzing employee data such as performance metrics, training history, and job experience and comparing that with publicly available data, AI-powered tools can provide insights into the skills and competencies that are most in demand within an organization. This approach is particularly useful for identifying skills gaps that are not immediately apparent, such as emerging skills or those that are in high demand but low supply.

Another method is the use of AI skills assessments. AI-powered skills assessments can provide a detailed picture of an employee's current skills and knowledge, highlighting areas where they may need further development. These assessments can also identify hidden talents and potential that may have been overlooked by traditional evaluation methods. Skills are transferable. AI can help us realize what skills are transferable to what roles.

Tools for Assessing Current Employee Skills and Knowledge

There are several AI-powered tools available to help organizations assess the skills and knowledge of their employees. These tools can range from simple skills tests to more sophisticated solutions that use machine learning algorithms to analyze employee data and provide targeted recommendations for training and development.

One example of an AI-powered skills assessment tool is Eightfold's Jobs Intelligence Engine. This is an AI-powered platform designed to help organizations identify and close skills gaps within their workforce. The platform uses machine learning algorithms to analyze employee data and job descriptions to identify the skills needed for each role, as well as any gaps between an employee's current skills and those required for their role.

The Jobs Intelligence Engine then provides personalized learning and development recommendations for each employee based on their specific skill gaps and learning preferences. The platform also offers insights into the current job market and trends, allowing organizations to stay up-to-date on the latest skills and job requirements.

One of the key features of the Jobs Intelligence Engine is its ability to provide personalized career path recommendations for employees. By analyzing an employee's skills, job history, and performance data, the platform can suggest potential career paths within the organization that align with their strengths and interests. This not only helps employees advance their careers but also ensures that the organization has a pipeline of skilled and motivated workers to fill critical roles.

Conclusion

In conclusion, artificial intelligence is proving to be a valuable tool for identifying skills gaps in organizations. By leveraging AI-powered platforms such as Eightfold's Jobs Intelligence Engine, businesses can quickly and accurately analyze their talent data to determine where they need to focus their upskilling efforts. This not only saves time and resources, but also ensures that training programs are aligned with the organization's actual needs, improving the effectiveness and impact of the upskilling initiatives.

The benefits of using AI in identifying skills gaps go beyond just data analysis. AI-powered platforms can also provide personalized recommendations for learning and development opportunities based on each employee's unique skill set and career aspirations. This can enhance employee engagement and motivation, leading to better retention rates and a more skilled and adaptable workforce.

However, it's important to note that AI should not replace human involvement in the upskilling process. While AI can provide valuable insights and recommendations, it's still up to human managers and leaders to develop and execute effective upskilling programs that address the organization's needs and align with its overall strategy. Additionally, the ethical implications of using AI in talent management must be considered and addressed to ensure fairness and avoid bias.

Overall, the combination of AI-powered platforms and human expertise and leadership can lead to a more effective and efficient upskilling process, resulting in a more skilled and adaptable workforce that is better equipped to meet the evolving needs of the business.

CHAPTER 5 - THE ROLE OF MANAGERS AND LEADERS IN UPSKILLING

In today's rapidly changing business environment, upskilling has become a critical aspect of workforce development. While there are many factors that contribute to the success of upskilling programs, the role of managers and leaders cannot be overstated. This chapter will explore the ways in which managers and leaders can create a culture of continuous learning, provide support for upskilling initiatives, and encourage employee buy-in and participation.

Strategies for building a culture of continuous learning

One of the most important roles that managers and leaders can play in upskilling is to build a culture of continuous learning within the organization. This involves creating an environment where employees are encouraged to take ownership of their own learning and development, and where ongoing training and development is seen as a key part of the company's overall strategy. To achieve this, managers and leaders can:

● Model the behavior they want to see: Managers and leaders should lead by example by continuously seeking out opportunities to learn and improve their own skills. This not only sets an example for their employees but also shows that they are committed to ongoing learning and development.

• Provide resources and support: Managers and leaders can help employees by providing access to resources such as training materials, online courses, and mentoring programs. They can also create opportunities for employees to attend conferences, workshops, and other learning events.

• Recognize and reward learning: Managers and leaders can encourage employees to take part in upskilling programs by recognizing and rewarding their efforts. This can be done through incentives such as promotions, bonuses, or special assignments.

The importance of leadership support for upskilling initiatives

Another key role that managers and leaders play in upskilling is to provide support for these initiatives. This includes:

• Making upskilling a priority: Managers and leaders need to make upskilling a priority within the organization by allocating the necessary resources and time to support these programs.

• Providing funding and resources: Managers and leaders can provide funding and resources to support upskilling programs. This includes investing in technology, hiring trainers, and providing time off for employees to attend training.

• Communicating the value of upskilling: Managers and leaders should communicate the value of upskilling to employees and stakeholders. They can do this by highlighting the benefits of upskilling programs, sharing success stories, and providing regular updates on the progress of these initiatives.

Techniques for encouraging employee buy-in and participation

Finally, managers and leaders can play a key role in encouraging employee buy-in and participation in upskilling programs. This can be achieved through:

• Soliciting employee input: Managers and leaders can solicit feedback from employees on the types of training and development programs they would like to see offered. This not only helps to ensure that the programs are relevant but also helps to build employee buy-in and ownership of the process.

• Providing support and encouragement: Managers and leaders can provide support and encouragement to employees who are participating in upskilling programs. This can be done through regular check-ins, providing feedback and coaching, and recognizing their progress and achievements.

• Creating a culture of learning: Managers and leaders can create a culture of learning by encouraging employees to share their knowledge and skills with one another. This not only helps to build a sense of community but also reinforces the idea that everyone has something to contribute and something to learn.

Conclusion

The role of managers and leaders in upskilling is critical for the success of any upskilling initiative. By building a culture of continuous learning, providing leadership support for upskilling initiatives, and encouraging employee buy-in and participation, organizations can create a workforce that is well-equipped to handle the demands of a rapidly changing business landscape.

Managers and leaders must understand that upskilling is

not a one-time event, but rather a continuous process that requires ongoing commitment and investment. By providing opportunities for employees to learn and grow, managers and leaders can create a culture of continuous improvement that benefits both employees and the organization as a whole.

Leadership support for upskilling initiatives is also essential. When leaders demonstrate a commitment to upskilling, it sends a powerful message to employees that investing in their skills and knowledge is a priority. This can help build trust and engagement among employees, leading to higher levels of motivation and performance.

Finally, managers and leaders must find ways to encourage employee buy-in and participation in upskilling initiatives. This can be achieved by clearly communicating the benefits of upskilling, providing incentives for participation, and creating a supportive learning environment that empowers employees to take ownership of their own learning.

Overall, the role of managers and leaders in upskilling cannot be overstated. By creating a culture of continuous learning, providing leadership support, and encouraging employee buy-in and participation, organizations can ensure that their workforce remains competitive and well-prepared for the challenges of the future.

CHAPTER 6 - DESIGNING EFFECTIVE TRAINING PROGRAMS

In order to upskill employees and close skills gaps, it is essential to design and deliver effective training programs. Training programs should be designed to meet the specific needs of the organization and its employees, and should incorporate a variety of techniques and strategies to ensure maximum engagement and retention of information. In this chapter, we will explore some techniques for designing and delivering effective training programs, as well as strategies for creating engaging and interactive learning experiences, best practices for incorporating technology in training, and tips for addressing different learning styles and preferences.

Techniques for Designing and Delivering Effective Training Programs

When designing a training program, it is important to consider the specific needs and goals of the organization and its employees.

4 techniques for designing and delivering effective training programs

1. Setting clear learning objectives: Clearly defined learning objectives help to ensure that the training program is focused and that employees know what

they are expected to learn.

2. Using a variety of teaching methods: Incorporating a variety of teaching methods, such as lectures, group discussions, case studies, and role-playing, can help to keep employees engaged and increase retention of information.

3. Providing feedback and reinforcement: Providing feedback and reinforcement, such as quizzes and assessments, can help to reinforce learning and ensure that employees are retaining the information presented in the training program.

4. Offering opportunities for practice and application: Providing opportunities for employees to practice and apply what they have learned, such as through simulations or on-the-job training, can help to solidify learning and increase the chances that employees will apply their new skills and knowledge in the workplace.

Strategies for Creating Engaging and Interactive Learning Experiences

In order to ensure maximum engagement and retention of information, it is important to create engaging and interactive learning experiences.

4 strategies for creating engaging and interactive learning experiences

1. Using real-world examples and scenarios: Using real-world examples and scenarios can help to make the training program more relevant to employees and increase their engagement with the material.

2. Encouraging participation and discussion: Encouraging participation and discussion, such as through group activities and discussions, can help

to increase engagement and foster a sense of community among employees.

3. Providing opportunities for feedback and reflection: Providing opportunities for feedback and reflection, such as through self-assessments and peer evaluations, can help employees to reflect on their learning and identify areas for improvement.

4. Incorporating multimedia and technology: Incorporating multimedia and technology, such as videos, interactive modules, and gamification, can help to make the training program more engaging and interactive.

Best Practices for Incorporating Technology in Training

Technology can be a powerful tool for delivering training programs, but it is important to use technology in a way that is effective and enhances the learning experience.

3 best practices for incorporating technology in training

1. Choosing the right technology: Choosing the right technology, such as learning management systems (LMS), video conferencing tools, and mobile learning apps, is essential for delivering effective training programs.

2. Providing clear instructions and support: Providing clear instructions and support for using technology is essential for ensuring that employees are able to access and use the technology effectively.

3. Ensuring accessibility and compatibility: Ensuring that the technology used in the training program is accessible and compatible with different devices and platforms is essential for ensuring that all

employees are able to participate in the training program.

Tips for Addressing Different Learning Styles and Preferences

Everyone has different learning styles and preferences, and it is important to address these differences in order to ensure that all employees are able to learn and benefit from the training program.

5 tips for addressing different learning styles and preferences

1. Incorporating visual, auditory, and kinesthetic learning methods: Incorporating a variety of learning methods can help accommodate different learning styles. Visual learners may benefit from diagrams, videos, and images, while auditory learners may prefer lectures, podcasts, and group discussions. Kinesthetic learners may benefit from hands-on activities and simulations.
2. Offering flexibility in learning: Providing flexibility in how employees can access and engage with the training program can also help accommodate different learning styles and preferences. For example, some employees may prefer to learn on their own time, while others may prefer to learn in a group setting.
3. Providing personalized learning experiences: Personalizing the learning experience for each employee can help cater to their specific needs and preferences. This can include creating customized learning plans, offering one-on-one coaching or mentoring, and providing opportunities for self-directed learning.
4. Encouraging collaboration and social learning:

Many employees benefit from collaborating with others and learning through social interactions. Encouraging group discussions, peer-to-peer learning, and team projects can help facilitate this type of learning.

5. Incorporating gamification and interactive elements: Gamification and interactive elements, such as quizzes, simulations, and games, can help make the learning experience more engaging and enjoyable for employees.

Conclusion

In conclusion, designing effective training programs that cater to different learning styles and preferences is crucial for the success of upskilling initiatives within organizations. It requires a thoughtful and strategic approach that takes into consideration the needs and preferences of all employees. By incorporating a variety of learning methods, such as visual, auditory, and kinesthetic, organizations can ensure that the training program is accessible to all employees.

Providing flexibility and personalizing the learning experience can also help employees to learn at their own pace and in their own way. Encouraging collaboration and social learning can create a sense of community and support among employees, while incorporating gamification and interactive elements can increase engagement and motivation.

Overall, designing effective training programs that cater to different learning styles and preferences is not only beneficial for individual employees but also for the organization as a whole. It can lead to improved employee satisfaction, increased productivity, and better business outcomes. Therefore, organizations should invest in designing and delivering training programs that are engaging, effective, and inclusive for all employees.

CHAPTER 7 - MEASURING THE ROI OF UPSKILLING

Investing in upskilling programs can yield significant benefits for organizations, such as increased productivity, employee satisfaction, and retention. However, to ensure that these programs are truly effective and provide a return on investment (ROI), it is crucial to measure their success. In this chapter, we will discuss key metrics for measuring the success of upskilling programs, tools and methods for tracking and analyzing the impact of training on business outcomes, and examples of successful upskilling initiatives and their ROI.

Key Metrics for Measuring the Success of Upskilling Programs
To measure the success of upskilling programs, organizations need to define and track key performance indicators (KPIs) that are directly related to the goals of the program.

4 common KPIs for upskilling programs include:

1. Employee engagement: Measuring the level of engagement and participation of employees in the training program is an important KPI, as it reflects the effectiveness of the program in capturing employees' interest and attention.
2. Skills improvement: Measuring the level of improvement in employees' skills and knowledge

is another important KPI, as it reflects the program's effectiveness in addressing skills gaps and enhancing employees' capabilities.

3. Job performance: Measuring the impact of upskilling programs on employees' job performance is an essential KPI, as it directly reflects the program's effectiveness in achieving business objectives and improving productivity.

4. Employee retention: Measuring the impact of upskilling programs on employee retention is another important KPI, as it reflects the program's effectiveness in enhancing employee satisfaction and loyalty.

Tools and Methods for Tracking and Analyzing the Impact of Training on Business Outcomes

To track and analyze the impact of training on business outcomes, organizations can use a variety of tools and methods.

4 tools to use to track and analyze the impact of training and development

1. Learning management systems (LMS): LMS platforms can provide detailed data and analytics on employee engagement, progress, and performance in the training program.

2. Surveys and assessments: Conducting pre- and post-training surveys and assessments can help measure the effectiveness of the training program and identify areas for improvement.

3. Performance evaluations: Incorporating performance evaluations into the upskilling program can help measure the impact of training on employees' job performance and productivity.

4. Business metrics: Measuring the impact of

upskilling programs on business metrics such as revenue, customer satisfaction, and employee turnover can help demonstrate the ROI of the program.

Examples of Successful Upskilling Initiatives and Their ROI

Many organizations have successfully implemented upskilling programs that have yielded significant ROI. Here are 5 anonymized examples of companies upskilling their teams and the gains they are receiving:

1. A manufacturing company invested in upskilling its employees in advanced data analytics and automation techniques. As a result, the company was able to improve its production processes, reduce waste, and increase efficiency. The upskilled employees were able to identify and troubleshoot issues more quickly, resulting in a 20% reduction in downtime and a 15% increase in production output. The company estimated a ROI of 5:1 based on the increased revenue and decreased costs.

2. A healthcare organization invested in upskilling its nursing staff in advanced patient care techniques, including the use of new technology tools. The organization saw significant improvements in patient outcomes, including a reduction in hospital readmissions and a decrease in patient complications. The upskilled nurses were also able to provide more efficient and effective care, resulting in a 10% reduction in patient care costs. The organization estimated a ROI of 3:1 based on the improved patient outcomes and reduced costs.

3. An online retailer implemented a training program to upskill their customer service representatives in

handling customer complaints more effectively. The program resulted in a 25% decrease in customer complaints and a 15% increase in customer satisfaction ratings. The ROI for the program was calculated to be 300%, with a payback period of 6 months.

4. A large financial institution invested in upskilling their sales team in effective negotiation techniques. After the program, the sales team closed 30% more deals and increased their average deal size by 20%. The ROI for the program was calculated to be 400%, with a payback period of 8 months.

5. A SaaS company introduced a training program to upskill their software engineers in new programming languages and technologies. As a result, the team was able to develop new software products more efficiently, resulting in a 50% reduction in development time and a 25% increase in revenue from software sales. The ROI for the program was calculated to be 500%, with a payback period of 4 months.

As you can clearly see, these examples demonstrate the significant ROI that can be achieved through effective upskilling programs. By measuring key metrics and analyzing the impact of training on business outcomes, organizations can ensure that their upskilling initiatives are not only effective, but also provide a positive return on investment. Imagine what your organization could achieve by upskilling their employees!

Conclusion

Measuring the ROI of upskilling programs is essential to ensure their effectiveness and justify the investment. By defining and tracking key performance indicators, using tools and methods to track and analyze the impact of training on business outcomes, and learning from successful upskilling initiatives and their

ROI, organizations can continuously improve their upskilling programs and maximize their impact on the business.

It is important to remember that ROI is not just about the financial returns, but also the overall impact on the organization and its employees. Successful upskilling initiatives can result in increased productivity, improved employee engagement and retention, better alignment with business goals, and a more agile and innovative workforce.

Additionally, organizations can leverage technology and data analytics to gain deeper insights into the effectiveness of their upskilling programs. By tracking employee progress and performance, identifying skill gaps and training needs, and evaluating the impact of training on business outcomes, organizations can continuously optimize their upskilling efforts and achieve even greater ROI.

In summary, measuring the ROI of upskilling programs requires a comprehensive approach that considers both financial and non-financial factors. Attrition rates and the cost to replace employees, to name a few, should all be taken into consideration when calculating your ROI. By investing in effective tracking and analysis tools, defining and tracking key metrics, and learning from successful upskilling initiatives, organizations can ensure that your upskilling programs are making a positive impact on the business and your employees.

CHAPTER 8 - OVERCOMING OBSTACLES TO UPSKILLING

Upskilling has become a critical component for organizations to remain competitive in today's rapidly changing business environment. However, despite the benefits of upskilling, many organizations face obstacles in implementing effective upskilling programs. In this chapter we will explore some of the common challenges organizations face when it comes to upskilling and provide strategies for overcoming these obstacles.You may be facing some of the same challenges in your organization. Have faith, many have traveled the path you are on before you. This chapter is focused on helping you overcome these challenges.

3 Common challenges to upskilling

1. Resistance to change

Resistance to change is a natural human reaction to new ideas, concepts, or practices. However, in the case of upskilling, it can pose a significant challenge to the success of the program. To overcome resistance to change, it is important to communicate the value of upskilling initiatives to employees and show them how it can benefit both them and the organization. Providing clear goals and objectives, along with a roadmap for achieving them, can also help to build employee motivation and engagement.

Another effective strategy for addressing resistance to change is to involve employees in the upskilling program's design and implementation process. By giving employees a voice in the process, they are more likely to feel invested in the program's success and motivated to participate. Organizations can also provide incentives, such as bonuses or promotions, for employees who successfully complete the upskilling program.

Another challenge that organizations face when implementing upskilling programs is a limited budget. Upskilling initiatives can be costly, especially for small businesses with limited resources. To overcome this challenge, organizations can explore cost-effective options for upskilling, such as online training courses, webinars, or peer-to-peer learning programs. Organizations can also consider partnering with local educational institutions or industry associations to access training programs and resources at a reduced cost.

Additionally, organizations can leverage existing resources and talent within the organization to create an internal upskilling program. This can be achieved by identifying employees with advanced skills and knowledge and tasking them with mentoring and training others. This approach can be particularly effective in creating a culture of continuous learning and upskilling within the organization.

In summary, while resistance to change and limited budgets are common challenges to upskilling initiatives, there are several strategies that organizations can use to overcome them. By involving employees in the process, exploring cost-effective options for upskilling, and leveraging existing resources and talent, organizations can create successful upskilling programs that benefit both employees and the organization.

2. Limited Budget

Limited budgets can pose a significant challenge for organizations when it comes to upskilling initiatives. However, there are several strategies that can be employed to manage upskilling programs on a limited budget.

One approach is to utilize internal resources and expertise. This can include identifying individuals within the organization who have the necessary skills and knowledge to act as trainers or mentors for other employees. By leveraging existing talent within the organization, it is possible to reduce the need for external training and associated costs.

Another strategy is to prioritize upskilling initiatives based on their impact on business outcomes. This involves identifying which skills are most critical for the organization's success and focusing upskilling efforts on those areas. This can help to ensure that limited resources are being used in the most effective way possible.

Organizations can also consider using technology-based training methods, such as e-learning or virtual training. These methods can be cost-effective and flexible, allowing employees to access training at their own pace and on their own schedule. Additionally, technology-based training can be easily updated and customized, ensuring that the training remains relevant and effective.

Finally, organizations can explore government-funded upskilling programs or partnerships with educational institutions. These programs can provide access to resources and training at a reduced cost or even for free. Additionally, partnerships with educational institutions can provide opportunities for employees to earn recognized certifications or degrees, enhancing their skills and credentials while minimizing the cost to the organization.

Limited budgets can pose a challenge to upskilling initiatives, but there are strategies that organizations can employ to manage these programs effectively. By utilizing internal resources, prioritizing critical skills, using technology-based training methods, and exploring partnerships and government-funded programs, organizations can offer effective upskilling programs that support their business goals without breaking the bank.

3. Time Constraints

Time constraints are a significant obstacle to upskilling, as organizations may struggle to find a way to provide training that is comprehensive and effective while also accommodating busy work schedules. It is essential to acknowledge that employees' time is valuable, and their productivity cannot be compromised for the sake of training. Therefore, organizations need to develop strategies to overcome this obstacle.

One approach to addressing time constraints is to offer flexible training options. This can include self-paced online courses or blended learning programs that combine in-person and online training. These options allow employees to complete training on their own schedule while also providing structure and support.

Another strategy is to integrate training into daily work tasks. This approach involves embedding training into the employees' work tasks, allowing them to learn new skills while completing their regular job duties. This approach can be particularly effective for on-the-job training and can help employees apply newly learned skills immediately in their work tasks.

Finally, organizations can provide employees with incentives for participating in upskilling programs. These incentives can be in the form of recognition, bonuses, promotions, or other forms of rewards. Such incentives can help to motivate employees to participate in training programs even when faced with time constraints.

Overall, time constraints can be a significant obstacle to upskilling, but organizations can overcome this challenge by offering flexible training options, integrating training into work tasks, and providing incentives for participation in training programs. By doing so, organizations can ensure that employees receive the necessary training while also maintaining productivity and efficiency in their work.

Strategies for overcoming obstacles to upskilling

Now that we have laid out some of the potential obstacles you might face, here are some tips for overcoming these obstacles.

1. Address the resistance to change

To effectively address resistance to change, organizations should prioritize clear communication and involvement of employees in the upskilling process. Communication should focus on the benefits of upskilling and how it can positively impact employees' career growth, job security, and the overall success of the organization. This can help employees understand the value of upskilling and motivate them to participate in training programs.

Involving employees in the design and delivery of upskilling programs can also increase their buy-in and motivation. Employees may have valuable insights on the specific skills and training that would be most beneficial to them, as well as preferences for how training is delivered. By soliciting employee input and involving them in the planning process, organizations can create upskilling programs that better meet the needs and interests of employees.

Another strategy for overcoming resistance to change is to make upskilling a part of the organization's culture. This involves creating a learning culture where continuous learning and development are encouraged and supported. Managers and leaders should lead by example and prioritize their own upskilling, and create opportunities for employees to share their knowledge and skills with others in the organization.

2. Use low-cost or free resources

One way for organizations to overcome limited budgets is by utilizing low-cost or free resources. Online learning platforms such as Coursera, Udemy, and LinkedIn Learning offer affordable training options with a variety of courses and topics. These platforms allow employees to access training on their own time and at their own pace, which can also help address time constraints. Furthermore, many of these platforms offer certifications that can provide employees with tangible evidence of their newly acquired skills.

Another way for organizations to address limited budgets is by creating mentorship programs. Pairing employees with more experienced colleagues who can share their knowledge and expertise can be an effective way to upskill employees without incurring significant costs. Mentorship programs also provide employees with opportunities for professional growth and networking.

In addition to online platforms and mentorship programs, organizations can encourage employees to attend conferences, workshops, and networking events related to their field. These events can provide employees with valuable knowledge and skills while also allowing them to connect with other professionals in their industry. While attending these events can come with costs such as registration fees or travel expenses, they can still be a more affordable option than comprehensive training programs.

Overall, by utilizing low-cost or free resources, creating mentorship programs, and encouraging attendance at industry events, organizations can overcome limited budgets and still provide valuable upskilling opportunities for their employees.

3. Offer flexible training options

Addressing time constraints can be challenging, but there are several strategies that organizations can use to ensure that employees are able to participate in upskilling programs without disrupting their work schedules. One effective approach is to offer flexible training options, such as online or self-paced learning. Online learning platforms can provide a range of training options that can be completed remotely, allowing employees to complete training at their own convenience. Self-paced learning can also help to ensure that employees can complete training on their own schedule and at their own pace.

Another strategy is to offer microlearning modules. Microlearning is an approach that breaks down complex training into small, bite-sized modules that can be completed quickly. This can be an effective way to deliver training that can easily fit into an employee's busy work schedule. Microlearning can also be delivered in a variety of formats, including videos, interactive simulations, and quizzes, making it a flexible and engaging option for upskilling.

In addition to these strategies, organizations can also consider scheduling training during off-hours or providing additional support to employees who are participating in upskilling programs. For example, organizations may offer incentives or rewards for completing training, provide coaching or mentoring support, or offer additional resources to help employees manage their workload while participating in training. By offering these types of resources and support, organizations can help to ensure that employees have the time and resources they need to participate in upskilling programs and develop new skills that can help them succeed in their roles.

3 tips for managing upskilling programs on a limited budget

1. Prioritize training needs

To manage upskilling programs on a limited budget, it's important to prioritize training needs based on the organization's strategic goals and objectives. This requires a thorough understanding of the skills and knowledge required to achieve those goals. By identifying the most critical skills and knowledge gaps, organizations can focus their resources on upskilling initiatives that will have the most significant impact.

In addition to prioritizing training needs, organizations can also consider investing in training programs that have a high return on investment (ROI). This means selecting training programs that are most likely to deliver the desired results for the organization. For example, training programs that focus on improving sales skills or increasing productivity may have a higher ROI than general professional development programs.

Another way to manage upskilling programs on a limited budget is to leverage existing resources. For instance, organizations can utilize in-house experts to deliver training sessions or develop training materials. This can help to reduce the cost of external training resources while still providing high-quality training.

Finally, it's important to track and measure the impact of upskilling programs on business outcomes. This allows organizations to demonstrate the value of their upskilling programs and make informed decisions about future investments. By continuously monitoring and evaluating the effectiveness of upskilling programs, organizations can make adjustments as needed to ensure maximum impact and ROI.

2. Leverage internal resources

Using internal resources can be an effective way to manage upskilling programs on a limited budget. By leveraging the knowledge and expertise of in-house trainers or subject matter experts, organizations can provide cost-effective training to employees. In-house trainers can be employees who have already received training and have expertise in a particular area. They can provide training to their colleagues and share their knowledge and experience.

Another approach is to encourage peer-to-peer training, where employees share their knowledge and skills with one another. This can be facilitated through formal mentoring programs, where experienced employees mentor and train new hires or junior staff. Peer-to-peer training can also be informal, where employees share knowledge and skills during team meetings or through online collaboration tools.

In addition to utilizing internal resources, organizations can also explore partnerships with educational institutions or industry associations. These partnerships can provide access to training programs or resources that may not be available internally. Additionally, organizations can consider offering tuition reimbursement programs to employees who pursue education or training outside of work.

Overall, managing upskilling programs on a limited budget requires creative thinking and prioritization of training needs. By leveraging internal resources, encouraging peer-to-peer training, and exploring partnerships with external organizations, organizations can provide cost-effective and impactful training programs to their employees.

3. Measure the impact of training

Measuring the effectiveness of upskilling programs is crucial to ensure that they are providing the desired outcomes and value for the organization. By tracking and analyzing key metrics, organizations can determine the impact of upskilling programs on employee performance, productivity, and retention. This information can be used to identify areas for improvement and make necessary adjustments to the training program.

4 Metrics to measure the effectiveness of upskilling programs

1. Employee performance: Measuring changes in employee performance is one of the most important metrics for assessing the effectiveness

of upskilling programs. This can include tracking changes in productivity, quality of work, and customer satisfaction. By analyzing these metrics, organizations can determine if upskilling programs are leading to improved employee performance.

2. Retention rates: High employee turnover can be costly for organizations. By tracking retention rates, organizations can determine if upskilling programs are helping to retain valuable employees. Retention rates can also be used to identify areas where additional upskilling may be needed.

3. Employee engagement: Employee engagement can be an indicator of the effectiveness of upskilling programs. Engaged employees are more likely to be motivated and productive, leading to better business outcomes. Surveys and feedback sessions can be used to gather information about employee engagement levels.

4. Training completion rates: Tracking the number of employees who complete upskilling programs can provide valuable information about the effectiveness of the training. Low completion rates may indicate that the training is not meeting the needs of employees or that the delivery method needs to be improved.

In addition to measuring key metrics, gathering feedback from employees is also essential. Regular feedback sessions can provide valuable insights into what is working well and what needs to be improved. Employees can provide suggestions for improving the training program and identify areas where additional upskilling may be needed.

I remember one of my first managers telling me, "If you can't measure something, you can't fix it". No truer words have ever been spoken to me in my career. Measuring the effectiveness of upskilling programs is essential for organizations to ensure that they are providing value and achieving desired outcomes. By tracking key metrics and gathering feedback from employees, organizations can identify areas for improvement and make necessary adjustments to the training program.

Conclusion

Like all change, upskilling can face numerous obstacles. With the right strategies and tactics, organizations and you can overcome them. Addressing resistance to change, using low-cost or free resources, offering flexible training options, prioritizing training needs, leveraging internal resources, and measuring the impact of training can all help ensure the success of upskilling programs. By overcoming these obstacles,you and your organizations can create a culture of continuous learning and stay ahead of the competition. You'll keep your best employees longer. You'll attract the best talent to your organization. You'll create an amazing workforce that people want to work for!

CHAPTER 9 -
THE FUTURE OF
UPSKILLING

Upskilling has become a critical component of workforce development, as organizations seek to remain competitive in a rapidly changing business landscape. As technology continues to advance and the workforce becomes increasingly diverse, organizations must adapt their upskilling programs to stay ahead of the curve. This chapter will explore emerging trends and innovations in upskilling, predictions for the future of workforce development, and opportunities and challenges for organizations and employees.

Emerging Trends and Innovations in Upskilling

One of the most significant trends in upskilling is the use of artificial intelligence (AI) and machine learning (ML) to personalize training programs. By using AI and ML algorithms, organizations can create customized training programs tailored to each employee's learning style, pace, and preferences. This approach can improve the effectiveness of upskilling programs and reduce the time and resources required for training.

Another trend is the use of immersive technologies, such as virtual reality (VR) and augmented reality (AR), to create more engaging and interactive training experiences. These technologies can simulate real-world scenarios, allowing employees to practice and apply new skills in a safe and controlled environment.

Predictions for the Future of Workforce Development

For this portion, I am going to use my proverbial crystal ball (oh how I wish I really had one). Since I work in this field, these are my personal predictions for the future of workforce development and what I am seeing on the horizon.

One of the most significant predictions I see is the rise of "micro-credentials" or "nano-degrees," which are shorter, more targeted training programs that focus on specific skills or knowledge. These credentials can be obtained through online learning platforms and are becoming increasingly recognized by employers as evidence of an individual's competence in a particular area.

Another prediction (I don't think this one will surprise anyone) is the continued growth of online and remote learning, as organizations seek to offer flexible training options to their employees. This trend was hyper-accelerated by the COVID-19 pandemic, which forced many organizations to shift to remote work and virtual training.

Opportunities and Challenges for Organizations and Employees

While upskilling presents numerous opportunities for both organizations and employees, there are also several challenges that must be addressed. One of the biggest challenges is the need for continuous learning, as technology and business practices continue to evolve. Organizations must commit to ongoing upskilling programs to ensure their employees have the skills and knowledge required to succeed.

The digital divide is a significant challenge that must be addressed when it comes to upskilling programs. While digital technologies are becoming increasingly important in the workplace, not all employees have access to the technology and tools required to participate in training programs. This can be particularly true for employees who live in rural areas or who come from low-income backgrounds.

To overcome this challenge, organizations must take steps to ensure that upskilling programs are accessible to all employees. This can include investing in technology and infrastructure to provide internet access and necessary hardware, such as computers or tablets to those in need. Additionally, organizations can offer mobile-friendly training options that can be accessed through smartphones, which can be more accessible for employees who do not have regular access to computers.

Moreover, it's essential to consider the socio-economic background of employees and provide additional support for those who face significant barriers to participation in training programs. For instance, organizations can offer financial assistance, scholarships, or grants to employees who may struggle to pay for training on their own. With inflation currently being as high as it is, you and your organization should consider collaborating with community organizations or government agencies to provide additional resources for employees facing barriers to upskilling.

By addressing the digital divide, organizations can ensure that all employees have access to the tools and technologies needed to participate in upskilling programs, regardless of their location or socio-economic background. This can help to promote equity and ensure that all employees have the opportunity to develop the skills and knowledge needed to succeed in the future of work. This is true DE&I work.

Conclusion

The future of upskilling presents exciting opportunities for organizations and employees to stay competitive and relevant in an ever-changing job market. Emerging trends and innovations are paving the way for new and improved methods of upskilling, making it easier and more accessible for individuals to learn and grow.

One such trend is the use of technology, including virtual and augmented reality, to create immersive learning experiences. This technology allows employees to practice new skills in a safe and controlled environment, increasing confidence and competence in their abilities. Online learning platforms and mobile apps are also becoming increasingly popular, offering flexible and convenient options for upskilling.

Another trend is the emphasis on soft skills, such as communication, leadership, and emotional intelligence. As automation and AI become more prevalent, these skills are becoming more important for individuals to differentiate themselves from machines and stay competitive in the job market. Upskilling programs that focus on developing these skills will become increasingly valuable in the future.

Predictions for the future of workforce development suggest that upskilling will become an even more critical aspect of business success. With the rapid pace of technological change and the need for organizations to remain agile and adaptable, upskilling will be essential for employees to keep up with the demands of their jobs. The rise of the gig economy and remote work will also require individuals to continuously upskill and be prepared for different job opportunities.

However, there are also challenges that must be addressed. One of the most significant challenges is the need for continuous learning. With the pace of technological change accelerating, individuals must be willing to learn and adapt throughout their entire career. This will require a cultural shift towards lifelong learning and a commitment to ongoing upskilling programs.

Another challenge is promoting inclusivity and accessibility. As mentioned earlier, the digital divide can create barriers to upskilling for some employees. Organizations must ensure that their upskilling programs are accessible to all employees, regardless of their socio-economic background or geographic location. Additionally, organizations must strive to create a culture of inclusivity and equity, ensuring that all employees have equal opportunities to learn and grow.

To wrap it all up, the future of upskilling is bright, with exciting opportunities for organizations and employees to stay competitive and adapt to changing market demands. However, it will require a commitment to ongoing learning and a focus on addressing challenges such as the digital divide and promoting inclusivity. By doing so, organizations can prepare for the future of work and ensure the continued success of their workforce.

CHAPTER 10 - CLOSING THOUGHTS

Throughout this book, we have explored the importance of upskilling in today's rapidly changing economy. We have discussed common challenges to upskilling, including resistance to change, limited budgets, and time constraints, and provided strategies for overcoming them. We have also examined emerging trends and innovations in upskilling and discussed the opportunities and challenges they present for organizations and employees.

One key takeaway is that upskilling is essential for organizations to remain competitive and adapt to changing market demands. It can help employees advance their careers, increase job security, and contribute to the success of the organization. Another takeaway is that upskilling programs must be accessible to all employees, regardless of their socio-economic background or geographic location.

Call to Action

As we look towards the future of work, it is critical that organizations and employees invest in upskilling. Organizations must commit to ongoing learning and prioritize upskilling programs that address critical skills gaps. They must also ensure that these programs are accessible to all employees, regardless of their background or location. Employees must take ownership of their career development and actively seek out opportunities to gain new skills and knowledge.

My Final Thoughts

Upskilling is a critical component of workforce development in today's rapidly changing economy. It's also the key to your organization's continued success in the markets you serve. As we have explored in this book, there are many benefits to investing in upskilling, including increased productivity, employee engagement, and organizational competitiveness. However, there are also significant challenges that must be addressed, such as resistance to change, limited budgets, and time constraints.

To overcome these challenges, organizations must prioritize upskilling as a strategic priority and commit to ongoing training programs. This includes addressing the digital divide and promoting inclusivity to ensure that all employees have access to training opportunities. Similarly, employees must also take ownership of their own career development by actively seeking out opportunities to learn and grow.

The key takeaway from this book is that upskilling is not just a one-time event but a continuous process. In today's economy, skills intelligence is more important than ever, and organizations and employees must be willing to embrace continuous learning to stay competitive. By investing in upskilling and promoting a culture of lifelong learning, organizations can ensure they have the skills needed to succeed in the future of work.

In light of this, my call to action for both organizations and employees is to make upskilling a top priority. Invest in training programs that address the skills gap, promote a culture of learning, and ensure that all employees have access to training opportunities. By doing so, we can create a skilled and adaptable workforce that is ready to meet the challenges of the future.

ABOUT THE AUTHOR

Michael Watason

About the Author Michael Watson is a talent acquisition expert and artificial intelligence enthusiast who is dedicated to using cutting-edge technologies to revolutionize the world of work. Michael's passion for work began in his early life, as he grew up with military parents who instilled in him the values of hard work, dedication, and service to others. His father dropped out of high school at 16 to join the Navy, and his mother served in both the Air Force and Marines, so Michael knows firsthand the importance of having a strong work ethic and a sense of purpose.

After years of experience in corporate HR and talent acquisition for companies such as Aerotek, Robert Half, Polycom, Western Digital, Workday, Rambus, and Gigamon, Michael joined the artificial intelligence startup Eightfold.ai. As a former customer of Eightfold.ai, he has unique first-hand knowledge of how AI is being used to hire and retain talent. At Eightfold, Michael is part of a team that is using AI for good, mapping skills to opportunities and enabling the right career for everyone in the world. As the Head of Global Customer Evangelism for Eightfold's products and solutions, Michael frequently interacts with business leaders, customer executives and government officials to amplify the power of Eightfold's artificial intelligence (AI) and their vision to use artificial intelligence for good and enable the right career for everyone in the world.

Michael believes that AI has the potential to help individuals find fulfilling and meaningful work, and he is dedicated to ensuring that everyone has access to the right career opportunities. He is passionate about helping individuals find work that aligns with their unique skills and interests, and he believes that AI can be a powerful tool to help people achieve their career goals.

Michael is a thought leader in the field of talent acquisition and artificial intelligence, and he is committed to using his expertise to help organizations and individuals navigate the rapidly changing world of work. He is the author of 2 books; Career AI: Navigating the Job Market in the Age of Artificial Intelligence and The AI-Powered HR Professional. He is a frequent speaker and writer on topics related to AI, talent acquisition, and career development, and he is always looking for new and innovative ways to use technology to improve people's lives.

Michael attended Fresno State University where he studied Criminology. When he is not working, Michael is busy working on his family's farm and dedicates a lot of time to coaching youth baseball and softball in his community. He is married and has two children.

BOOKS BY THIS AUTHOR

Career Ai: Navigating The Job Market In The Age Of Artificial Intelligence

This book, written by Michael R. Watson, covers a wide range of topics related to artificial intelligence (AI) and its impact on the job market, personal life, and society as a whole. Raised by military parents who served in the Air Force, Marines, and Navy, Michael has gained a unique perspective on the importance of adapting to change and being open to new opportunities throughout his life and career.

After working in corporate HR and talent acquisition for over 20 years for companies such as Aerotek, Robert Half, Polycom, Western Digital, Workday, Rambus, and Gigamon, Michael made a career move joined an AI startup called Eightfold.ai, which is dedicated to mapping skills to opportunities by using AI the level the career playing field. As a former customer of Eightfold, he has first-hand knowledge of how AI is being used to hire and retain talent for the largest corporations around the world.

The book covers a variety of topics, including ethical considerations for AI-enabled careers, strategies for building a personal brand in the digital age, and tips for navigating the global job market with AI. Michael also explores the intersection of AI and creativity, the role of emotional intelligence in the age of AI, and the challenges and opportunities presented by the gig economy. AI is here to stay and this book serves as a guide to help you navigate your career in the age of artificial intelligence.

In addition to his professional work, Michael is also active in his community, coaching youth baseball and softball and dedicating time to his family's farm. The book highlights the importance of finding a work-life balance in the digital age, and provides insights into how AI can be used to create a more fulfilling and meaningful life.

Overall, the book is a comprehensive guide to navigating the rapidly changing landscape of work and technology, and provides practical advice and strategies for adapting to the future of AI.

The Ai-Powered Hr Professional: How To Further Your Career In Hr By Embracing Artificial Intelligence

This book explores the transformative potential of AI in the field of human resources. The conversation covers a wide range of topics, including recruitment, employee engagement, compensation and benefits, learning and development, succession planning, and managing gig workers. Each chapter provides an overview of how AI can be used to improve HR practices, case studies of companies that have successfully used AI in these areas, and best practices for using AI in a way that is fair, transparent, and aligned with the company's overall goals and values.

Throughout the conversation, key points are highlighted, including the importance of using diverse data sets to train AI algorithms, involving diverse groups of employees in the development and implementation of AI-based solutions, balancing the use of technology with a human touch, and ensuring that AI is used in a way that is fair, transparent, and compliant with relevant laws and regulations. The potential of AI to drive innovation and growth in the HR industry is emphasized, as well as the need for HR professionals and companies to embrace AI and use it to advance their careers and drive business success.

Overall, this book provides a comprehensive and practical guide to using AI in HR, showcasing the transformative potential of this technology in improving HR practices and ultimately driving business success. It is a must-read for HR professionals and business leaders who are interested in staying ahead of the curve in this rapidly evolving field.

www.ingramcontent.com/pod-product-compliance
Lightning Source LLC
Chambersburg PA
CBHW070515220526
45467CB00002B/677